DELIGHTFUL
Desserts

DELIGHTFUL

Desserts

Marlene van der Westhuizen

ACKNOWLEDGEMENTS

This little book of dessert recipes for all the lovely girls in our extended family.
Elena, Michela, Lisa, Petro, Anja, Jana, Emma and Amelia, I hope all of you can use this book to great effect for the rest of your lives. Enjoy!

Thank you to Basil van Rooyen, Louise Grantham, René de Wet and the photographers Stephen Inggs, Gerda Genis and Jan-Hendrik van der Westhuizen. It was, as always, a pleasure to work with you.

ISBN: 978-1-920434-21-2
First edition, first impression 2011

Published jointly by Bookstorm (Pty) Limited, Suite 10, Private Bag X12, Cresta, 2118, Johannesburg, South Africa,
www.bookstorm.co.za
and Pan Macmillan South Africa, Private Bag X19, Northlands, 2116, Johannesburg, South Africa,
www.panmacmillan.co.za

Distributed by Pan Macmillan Via Booksite Afrika

Photography by Stephen Inggs, Gerda Genis and Jan-Hendrik van der Westhuizen
Edited by Content by Design
Proofread by Patricia Botes
Cover design by René de Wet
Design and layout by René de Wet
Printed and bound by Ultra Litho (Pty) Limited

Contents

Preface

And then we serve dessert.

Following hot on the heels of my most recent books, *Lazy Lunches* and *Decadent Dinners*, it was a complete pleasure to compile this sturdy handful of delightful desserts.

I have been wafting around in clouds of flour and sugar these past months, testing and playing with recipes to add to the existing ones from my two earlier books, *Delectable* and *Sumptuous*.

In an effort to make it a whole lot easier for you to make up your mind about what dessert to serve when, I have decided to stick to the not-so-original but oh-so-practical order of the seasons.

I hope you just adore this little book full of family and friends' recipes. It certainly was a pleasure to put it together!

Marlene van der Westhuizen
Cape Town, 2011

Spring

Strawberries and cream will always epitomise spring. In the little village of Charroux in France we have a small bed of tulips that push out beautiful deep-red and dark-purple blooms at the beginning of the European spring. Around their feet grow the sweetest of wild strawberries that I love picking, warm from the sun, to bake in little tarts with large dollops of Mascarpone.

And then there is the all-time favourite of many generations of schoolboys, Eton mess – a delicious heap of a pudding that lures you back again and again to dip your spoon just one more time.

Enjoy these fabulously light and gently sweet spring desserts. And perhaps add a glass of bubbly as a salute to the long, sun-filled days to come.

Bella's cheesecake

Let's just do the crust the usual way, by crunching up a packet of shortbread biscuits and stirring the crumbs into 75 ml of melted unsalted butter. Line a greased baking tin with the crumb mixture and keep in the fridge until you need it. Bella's cheesecake filling is the best I can remember from my childhood days.

- 3 eggs
- 125 g castor sugar
- 500 ml smooth cream cheese
- 125 ml double cream

Preheat the oven to 160 deg C/Gas 3. Whip the eggs and castor sugar until foamy. Spoon the cream cheese into the mixture and whip thoroughly. Fold in the cream. Pour the mixture into the crust and bake for 40 minutes.

When the cake has risen and set, turn off the oven and open the oven door. Allow the cake to cool in the oven. Serve in thick slices and burst into song!

Champagne jelly with berries

A festive and wonderfully light dessert for a spring lunch in the Mother City ... or anywhere else, for that matter.

- 750 ml Champagne
- 5 gelatine leaves, soaked in a little water
- 400 g mixed berries

Gently heat the Champagne and add the gelatine leaves. Stir until the leaves have melted completely. Remove from the heat.

Arrange some of the berries in four jelly moulds and pour enough of the liquid over the berries to just cover them. Place in the fridge for as long as it takes the jelly to set. Keep the rest of the liquid outside the fridge.

Remove the moulds from the fridge and repeat the process until you have used all the berries and Champagne.

Leave the jellies in the fridge until you need them. Dip the moulds in warm water for a moment before you tip them over onto the serving plates. They will gradually ease their way down!

Great with, naturally, a glass of Champagne and, if you wish, a little coulis of puréed fruit.

Griet's banana bread

Most of us grew up with some variation of banana bread. The smell of it baking will always be comforting.

- 125 g butter, plus extra for greasing
- 250 g castor sugar
- 2 eggs
- 1 t vanilla paste
- 3 large bananas, peeled and mashed
- 500 g self-raising flour
- 100 g walnuts, chopped

Preheat the oven to 180 deg C/Gas 4. Butter a bread pan well.*

Cream the butter and castor sugar until it is light in colour and foamy. Add the eggs, one at a time, and beat well. Add the vanilla paste. Fold the bananas and the flour into the egg mixture. Blend well and add the walnuts to the mixture. Scrape the dough into the bread pan.

Bake the bread for 45 minutes or until a skewer comes out dry. Allow to cool slightly in the pan before turning it out onto a cooling rack.

* I also enjoy playing with this cake by baking little individual breads in clay moulds.

Pavlova with strawberry syrup

What a lovely alternative to the normal pavlova. Hubert Maetz, a French chef with whom I've spent some time in the Alsace, always trained us by pointing out the 'cinema' factor ... he would love this!

Meringue
- 350 g egg whites
- 450 g castor sugar
- 1 T cornflour
- 1 t vanilla paste
- butter for greasing

Recipe continues overleaf

Meringue

Preheat the oven to 220 deg C/Gas 7. Beat the egg whites until they form soft peaks. Take care not to whip them until they dry out – that will make the cooked pavlova brittle.

Add half of the meringue castor sugar to the egg whites, spoon by spoon, beating all the time. Add the cornflour and then fold the rest of the pavlova castor sugar into the mixture. Make sure the sugar has dissolved. Finally, add one teaspoon of vanilla paste.*

Spoon the mixture into a large metal or ovenproof tray lined with buttered paper. I usually smear some unsalted butter over the buttered paper as well. Shape the meringue into a small circular pavlova ... try to get as much height as possible, and to form a little 'hill' right in the middle of the pavlova that is not higher than the sides.

Place in the oven and immediately reduce the heat to 140 deg C/Gas 2. Bake for about two hours. The pavlova will rise slowly and turn a light caramel colour with a crisp meringue look. The inside will be light and fairycake-like. Remove from the oven and allow it to cool.

* See page 157

continues overleaf

Pavlova with strawberry syrup

continued

Syrup
- 750 ml white wine
- 250 g castor sugar
- 1 punnet strawberries, unhulled
- 1 t vanilla paste
- 300 ml thick cream to serve

Syrup

Bring the wine and syrup castor sugar to a fast boil in a deep pot, and let it reduce to a syrupy consistency. Add two strawberries to the syrup. Add one teaspoon of vanilla paste and allow the mixture to cool.

Whip the cream until it forms soft peaks.

Just before serving, remove the strawberries from the syrup, which will be a lovely pink colour. Spoon the cream onto the cooled pavlova, heap the fresh strawberries on top of the cream, and spoon the lovely pink syrup over the strawberries.

Soufflé Grand Marnier

My neighbour in Charroux, Marie-Chantel Bardet, serves this soufflé with great success to her guests ... and sometimes to us if we're lucky!

- butter for greasing
- 3 eggs, separated
- 70 g castor sugar
- 1 T Grand Marnier

Preheat the oven to 250 deg C/Gas 9. Butter eight soufflé ramekins well.

Combine the egg yolks with the castor sugar and whip until light and creamy. Add the Grand Marnier and blend in thoroughly.

Whip the egg whites separately until they form a soft foam. Fold the foamy whites into the Grand Marnier mixture and gently divide among the ramekins. Bake in the really hot oven for about four minutes, and serve immediately.

Peach & caramel tarts

In spring, with its abundance of fresh fruit, this is one of the handiest recipes around. Using a huge variety of soft fruit I am constantly churning out these little pastries. I use any fruit, from apples to peaches, pears and prunes. Enjoy!

- 100 g butter, melted
- 250 g sugar
- 125 ml water
- 125 ml crème fraîche plus extra to serve
- 125 g unsalted butter
- 1 sheet puff pastry, thawed
- 6 peaches, each cut into six wedges
- 6 sprigs thyme

Preheat the oven to 220 deg C/Gas 7. Butter 6 individual shallow flan dishes.

Combine the sugar with 125 ml water in a saucepan, and cook over high heat until it turns a caramel colour. Add the crème fraîche, whisking vigorously. Be careful of the steam! Remove from the heat, cut the butter into small pieces and whisk into the caramel.

Prepare the pastry cases by rolling open the puff pastry and cutting each sheet into six blocks with a sharp knife. Place the pastry blocks into the buttered moulds. Arrange the peach wedges in the cases.

Pour the caramel over the peach wedges and bake for about 15 minutes until the pastry is slightly browned. Serve with a dollop of crème fraîche and a sprig of thyme for garnish.

Pistachio cake with Noble Late Harvest

Serves 10

A lovely classic to have in your repertoire. I love baking these old favourites.

- butter for greasing
- 6 eggs
- 175 g castor sugar
- 1 T orange zest
- 125 ml Noble Late Harvest wine
- 100 ml olive oil
- pinch of salt
- 150 g self-raising flour
- 125 g unsalted pistachios, chopped, plus extra for sprinkling
- icing sugar for dusting

Preheat the oven to 180 deg C/Gas 4. Line a medium-sized cake tin with baking paper, greasing it well.*

Separate the eggs, and beat the yolks with the castor sugar until pale and fluffy. In a separate bowl, whisk the egg whites until stiff. Fold the zest, wine, olive oil, salt, flour, nuts and egg whites into the yolk mixture.

Pour the mixture into the cake tin and bake for about 20 minutes. Then reduce the heat to 100 deg C/Gas ½ and bake for another 20 minutes.

Remove from the oven and allow to cool before removing from the tin. The cake will deflate a little, like a soufflé. Lovely! Dust with the icing sugar and sprinkle with some more pistachios.

* *I actually prefer baking this in a ring tin. It has such a festive air!*

Strawberries with Hanepoot

And how good is this! If you cannot get your hands on some Hanepoot, use a sweet, mature sherry.

- 500 g ripe strawberries, hulled and sliced
- 50 g icing sugar
- 250 ml Hanepoot
- ½ t matured balsamic vinegar
- freshly ground black pepper
- 350 ml rich, thick yoghurt
- 150 ml golden honey

Place the strawberries in a mixing bowl and sprinkle the icing sugar over them. Allow them to rest until the icing sugar has melted away. Add the Hanepoot and the balsamic vinegar to the bowl, and leave the strawberries to soak for at least an hour.

Spoon the strawberries into individual serving bowls and give each bowl a sprinkling of black pepper. Add a dollop of yoghurt to each portion and garnish with a dribble of honey before serving. Delicious!

Tiramisu with melted white chocolate

To add more decadence to an already seriously rich dessert, I thought this idea of adding a soupçon of creamy white chocolate sauce was stunning!

- 600 g good-quality white chocolate
- 2 eggs, separated
- 75 g castor sugar
- 250 g Mascarpone
- 100 ml espresso
- 25 ml Cognac
- 30 savoiardi biscuits (finger biscuits)
- 125 ml fresh cream

Grate 200 g of the white chocolate and keep aside. Beat the yolks with the castor sugar until frothy. Beat the egg whites until they form soft peaks, and fold them into the yolk mixture together with the Mascarpone.

Pour the espresso and Cognac into a flat dish. Dip the biscuits quickly into the liquid before placing them in alternative layers with the Mascarpone and egg mixture in a serving dish.

Meanwhile, melt the rest of the chocolate over a double boiler. Fold the cream into the chocolate to create a creamy sauce, and spoon it over the tiramisu. Garnish with grated chocolate and serve.

Berry tarts with Mascarpone

This dessert was born out of sheer desperation when confronted with an almost empty fridge … just a forgotten roll of puff pastry and a tub of Mascarpone a second away from its sell-by date! The berries were hunted down in the garden … you don't need many.

- 1 sheet puff pastry, thawed
- 120 g castor sugar
- 250 g Mascarpone
- vanilla to taste
- berries of choice
- 125 ml double cream to serve

Preheat the oven to 180 deg C/Gas 4. Cut and mould the puff pastry into flan ramekins.

Fold the castor sugar into the Mascarpone. Add the vanilla, and fold a handful of berries into the cheese mixture. Wild strawberries are great! Put a dollop in each ramekin and bake for around 20 minutes.

Remove from the oven and add some fresh berries. Serve with a scoop of double cream.

Panna cotta with basil

Panna cotta is a universally loved dessert. A little touch of basil from the garden adds to the spring feel.

- 350 ml full-cream milk
- 250 ml single cream
- 1 t vanilla paste
- 125 g castor sugar
- 2 gelatine leaves
- 125 ml double cream
- 6 fresh basil leaves

Put the milk, single cream, vanilla and castor sugar into a pot and bring to the boil. Remove from the heat and fold in the gelatine. Stir until the leaves have melted. Strain the mixture through a sieve and allow it to cool.

Stir a little of this mixture into the double cream before gently adding the double cream to the milk mixture, and then strain again. Place a fresh basil leaf at the bottom of each mould and then pour the panna cotta into the moulds.

Chill until set. Turn out onto individual plates to serve.

Bambi's baked custard

Bambi Rose is an old friend of my parents. This recipe of hers cannot fail, and it's delicious!

- 825 g sugar
- 125 ml water
- butter for greasing
- 1 t vanilla paste
- 6 eggs, whipped until foamy
- 1.5 l milk, lightly heated

Preheat the oven to 180 deg C/Gas 4. Dissolve 750 g of the sugar in 125 ml water and boil gently until it reaches a brown, syrupy consistency. Pour the syrup into a buttered bread tin.* Allow the syrup to cool.

Add the vanilla paste and the rest of the sugar (75 g) to the eggs, and whip well. Fold the egg mixture into the slightly warm milk. Pour the custard very slowly through a sieve onto the syrup in the buttered bread tin.

Bake the custard in a bain-marie for about 15 minutes. Then turn the heat down to 120 deg C/ Gas 1 and bake until set. This normally takes about 30 minutes. Do remember that it will still be slightly wobbly even if it has set!

Allow the custard to cool before gently tipping it onto a serving dish. Serve in slices.

* I also use individual moulds. Lovely!

Eton Mess

I believe that the colonies were probably founded on this!

- 6 small meringues
- 250 ml cream
- 1 t vanilla paste
- 250 g strawberries, sliced into quarters

Break the meringues into bite-sized bits in a bowl. Whip the cream until it forms soft peaks. Add the vanilla to the cream and blend lightly. Fold the cream gently into the meringues. Add the strawberries and spoon the mixture into separate pudding bowls. Serve!

White peach & basil compote

A delightful spring dessert.

- 125 g sugar
- 250 ml sweet white wine
- 1 t vanilla paste
- 1 T honey
- 4 cling peaches, peeled and sliced (not too thinly)
- handful fresh basil leaves, roughly chopped
- vanilla ice cream to serve

Using a non-stick wok or rounded pan, dissolve the sugar in the wine, and then add the vanilla paste. Allow the syrup to reduce to 'big bubble' stage before adding both the honey and the peach slices. Cook for about three minutes while stirring gently.

Remove from the heat, add the freshly chopped basil leaves and serve immediately with a dollop of vanilla ice cream.

Macadamia & Stroh rum cake

Serves 10

This is a tip of the hat to the northern part of South Africa where the most delicious macadamia nuts are harvested.

- 125 g macadamia nuts, roasted and finely chopped
- 200 g butter, room temperature, plus extra for greasing
- 200 g castor sugar
- 4 eggs
- 2 T Stroh rum
- 1 t vanilla paste
- 150 g self-raising flour, plus extra for flouring

Recipe ontinues overleaf

Preheat the oven to 180 deg C/Gas 4. Butter and flour a round cake tin and sprinkle the base with some of the nuts.

Beat the butter and castor sugar together until fabulously foamy. Add the eggs, Stroh rum and vanilla paste, and mix well. Mix the flour and nuts together and spoon into the egg mixture. Fold together gently and pour into the cake tin.

Bake for about 40 minutes or until a skewer comes out clean. Allow the cake to cool in the tin before turning it out onto a cooling rack.

Serve with the cheesy cream mixture on the following page.

continues overleaf

Cheesy cream

- 125 ml crème fraîche
- 25 ml cream cheese
- 75 g icing sugar, sifted

Spoon all the ingredients together and whisk until it has a smooth, creamy consistency. This is delicious with all kinds of cakes and fruit tarts. Enjoy!

Molten chocolate puddings with white centre

By now this is a classic dessert. As far as I know, it originated with the Roux brothers. To add some zing, I've come up with the idea of placing a small block of soft-centred white Lindt chocolate into the middle of each mould before baking the puddings. The result is spectacular! Start the day before.

- 5 eggs, plus 5 extra yolks
- 125 g unrefined castor sugar
- 250 g bitter, dark chocolate (at least 70% cocoa), broken into pieces
- 250 g unsalted butter, plus extra for greasing
- 50 g plain flour, sifted
- 8 blocks soft-centred white chocolate

In a bowl, beat together the eggs, yolks and castor sugar until pale. Meanwhile, melt the chocolate and butter gently in a bowl set over a pan of hot water. Remove from the heat.

Slowly add the chocolate to the egg mixture, beating until smooth. Fold in the flour. Pour into buttered moulds before the mixture begins to firm up. Put a block of white chocolate into the middle of each. Chill overnight.

The next day, heat the oven to 180 deg C/ Gas 4. Bake for about 10 to 15 minutes until the centres 'puff' and look dry. Turn out and serve.

Summer

Cherries and blueberry pie are what it's all about on the fabulously warm days of seemingly endless summer. Mountains of gloriously glossy deep-red cherries, jewel-like blueberries and magnificent Cape grapes.

I know we're heading for summer when I get trapped behind the first heavily laden harvest trucks, groaning with freshly picked grapes, on the Faure Road towards Stellenbosch!

I hope you just love preparing these refreshing desserts while sipping an old-fashioned Champagne cocktail.

Blueberry pie

This is a spectacularly easy pie to make. I love the way the glossy berries pop in your mouth when you bite into them!

- 1 sheet puff pastry, thawed
- butter for greasing
- 3 eggs
- 3 T castor sugar
- 200 ml cream plus extra to serve
- 1 kg fresh blueberries

Preheat the oven to 220 deg C/Gas 7. Roll the pastry to fit a 23 cm pie plate or individual moulds. Butter the pie plate or moulds, and line them with the pastry.

Beat the eggs with the castor sugar and fold the cream into the mixture. Fill the pastry with the blueberries and pour the creamy mixture over the berries.

Bake for about 25 minutes or until the filling has set. Allow to cool and serve with a dollop of cream.

White chocolate mousse

The sexiest little mousse imaginable!

- 3 x 100 g slabs of white Lindt chocolate
- 375 ml cream
- 2 t vanilla paste
- 1 bottle light white wine
- 500 g castor sugar
- 16 strawberries (2 per person)
- Raspberries optional

Place the chocolate in a heat-resistant bowl and melt in a microwave at the lowest power for 30 seconds at a time, stirring frequently, until the chocolate is nice and smooth.

In the meantime, beat the cream until it forms soft peaks. Stir in the vanilla paste.* Stir the melted chocolate into the cream mixture with a spoon, and spoon the mixture into pretty glasses. Leave in a cool place (not the fridge!).

Boil the wine and castor sugar until it is syrupy. Quickly dip the strawberries into the syrup and arrange them on serving plates, alongside the glasses of mousse. Drizzle with the wine syrup. Finger-licking is totally allowed!

* See page 157

Peaches in white wine syrup with Roquefort

Cooking these peaches is one of the most delightful things to do – a little like alchemy ...

- 375 ml dry white wine
- 250 g castor sugar
- 1 t vanilla paste
- 6 rosy-cheeked peaches
- 6 thin slices of Roquefort

Bring the wine and castor sugar to a gentle boil in a pot that's big enough to hold all six peaches, ideally in one layer. Add the vanilla paste. Once the sugar has dissolved, place the unpeeled peaches in the pot. *

Allow the peaches to simmer until they are soft, then remove them and place them in the fridge. Continue boiling the liquid until it has a syrupy consistency.

Remove the peaches from the fridge just before serving and peel them. The peels should slip off beautifully. Place each peach on a plate with a slice of Roquefort. Spoon a little of the syrup over each peach and slice of cheese.

* *Boiling the peaches with their peels on turns the syrup a lovely pink colour.*

Blinis aux Jardins des Thévenets

I have my friend Lynn to thank for this easy way to sort out that most versatile of dessert basics, the blini.

- 125 ml plain yoghurt, natural or Bulgarian
- equal amount of self-raising flour (use the empty yoghurt cup to measure)
- 1 egg
- 1 T oil

Mix all the ingredients together in a small bowl and set aside for 20 minutes. Heat a heavy-bottomed frying pan, add just a drop of oil, and spoon tablespoons of batter into the pan. As soon as bubbles start appearing, flip over and do the other side.

You'll probably find that you can do five or six at a time in an average-sized pan – by the time you've spooned in the last one, the first one is ready to be flipped.

Serve with cream or yoghurt and fresh berries.

Nougat cake

This is a really easy but spectacular dessert to treat friends with. Enjoy!

- 100 g dates, seeded and chopped
- 100 g Boudoir biscuits, cut into 1 cm pieces
- 100 g pecan nuts, chopped
- 4 egg whites, whipped
- 250 g castor sugar
- ½ t vanilla extract
- butter for greasing
- 350 ml cream, whipped
- preserved fruit and chocolate shavings for garnish

Preheat the oven to 160 deg C/Gas 3. Fold together the dates, biscuits and pecan nuts. Combine the egg whites, castor sugar and vanilla extract, and mix until it has a creamy consistency. Gently fold the date mixture into this.

Butter a baking sheet, spoon the mixture onto it and spread it evenly. Bake for 30 minutes and then allow it to cool.

Slice the nougat in half. Spoon half of the cream onto one half of the nougat, and place the other half of the nougat on top. Spoon the rest of the cream on top and garnish with the preserved fruit and chocolate shavings. Serve in slices. Delicious!

Cherry clafoutis

Clafoutis hails from the Limousin area of France and traditionally consists of black cherries arranged in a buttered dish, covered with a thickish batter and baked. We only wash and stalk the cherries and never remove the pips ... they add their flavour to the batter during cooking. A wonderfully light cake that can happily be enjoyed with a glass of ice-cold rosé.

- 1 T butter for greasing
- 250 g cake flour
- 125 g castor sugar
- pinch of salt
- 4 eggs
- 1 t vanilla paste
- 500 ml boiled milk, cooled
- 2 T Stroh rum
- 750 g cherries*
- icing sugar for dusting

Preheat the oven to 200 deg C/Gas 6. Butter a pie dish or any other pretty ovenproof container.

Mix together the flour, castor sugar and salt. Beat in the eggs, one at a time, and add the vanilla. Using a spatula, fold in the milk and rum.

Distribute the cherries evenly on the bottom of the dish. Pour the batter over the fruit and bake for about 35 minutes. Dust with icing sugar before serving warm or cooled.

* Also lovely with peeled and sliced pears or peaches, and with prunes.

Banana frangipane

This is an easy tart to bake if you're in a hurry!

- butter for greasing
- 1 sheet of shortcrust pastry
- 125 g almonds, crushed and lightly roasted
- 3 bananas, peeled and sliced into strips
- 2 eggs, whipped
- 125 ml cream
- 75 g castor sugar
- 1 t vanilla paste
- 75 g flaked almonds, roasted

Preheat the oven to 180 deg C/Gas 4. Butter a tart mould and line with the pastry. Sprinkle the crushed almonds over the bottom of the pastry, covering it completely.

Arrange the banana strips, slightly overlapping, on top of the almonds. Gently whisk together the eggs, cream, castor sugar and vanilla paste.

Spoon this creamy mixture over the bananas and put in the oven for about 30 minutes.

Allow the tart to cool slightly, sprinkle with the almond flakes and serve.

Champagne sabayon

Serves 8

I normally spoon the sabayon over any fresh fruit or berries I can lay my hands on. My husband loves hearing the tack-tack of the whisk and normally opens a bottle of Champagne on cue!

- 5 egg yolks
- 4 T castor sugar
- 1 t vanilla paste
- juice of 1 lemon
- 150 ml Champagne
- berries to serve

Whisk the egg yolks, castor sugar, vanilla paste, lemon juice and Champagne in a bowl over a pan of boiling water. Take care not to let the base of the bowl touch the water.

Once the mixture is thick and creamy, spoon it over berries of your choice. Serve immediately.

Grape & fennel seed tart

I enjoy preparing this during harvest time ... for obvious reasons.

- butter for greasing
- 1 sheet puff pastry, thawed
- 1 egg white
- 2 whole eggs, whipped
- 125 ml crème fraîche
- 1 T castor sugar
- 1 t vanilla paste
- 400 g red grapes, seeded and halved
- 1 T fennel seeds
- thick cream to serve

Preheat the oven to 220 deg C/Gas 7. Line six greased, loose-bottomed (totally love this word ... and can't imagine why!) flan pans with the pastry, prick the dough with a fork and brush lightly with a little egg white. This prevents the dough from becoming soggy.

Fold together the eggs, crème fraîche, castor sugar and vanilla paste.* Distribute the grape halves among the pastry bases and spoon the creamy mixture over the grapes.

Sprinkle with the fennel seeds and slide into the oven for about 25 minutes or until the pastry is a lovely caramel colour. Serve still piping hot with a dollop of thick cream.

* See page 157

Ricotta dessert with Cognac & citrus zest

I found this recipe years ago in a magazine, and it was attributed to a gentleman named Ron. Thanks Ron!

- 250 g castor sugar
- 75 ml water
- 250 ml Cognac
- zest of 1 lemon, 1 lime and 1 orange
- 1 t vanilla paste
- 500 g Ricotta
- 100 g pistachios, lightly roasted

Use a small cooking pot and melt the castor sugar in 75 ml water. Add the Cognac and the three types of zest, and reduce over a low heat until the lemon, lime and orange peel is beautifully glazed and translucent. (Take care that the mixture does not reduce too much and crystallise. Add a little water if necessary.) Stir the vanilla paste into the syrup.

Place the entire piece of ricotta on a slightly hollow serving plate and spoon the syrup over the cheese. Arrange the glistening zest on top, and toss the pistachios over the cheese just before serving.

Lovely with an oat biscuit and, of course, a snifter of Cognac or brandy.

Berry cocktail with Champagne

This is one of those really silly and timeless cocktails that probably hails from the sixties. Or earlier? Fantastic on a hot summer day!

- 180 g castor sugar
- 2 T water
- 200 g raspberries
- 200 g blackberries
- 1 bottle Champagne, well chilled

In a small skillet and over medium heat, melt 80 g of the castor sugar in 2 T water, add half of the raspberries and cook until a lovely syrup forms. The raspberries will have turned the syrup a festive pink. Allow the syrup to cool a bit and pour it through a strainer. Discard the berries.

Place the remaining castor sugar on a plate. Dip the rims of six glasses in the syrup and then into the sugar for decoration. Carefully fill the glasses with the rest of the berries. Pour the syrup equally into the six glasses and over the berries.

Place the glasses on a tray and refrigerate until you want to pour in the Champagne. When you do, don't fill the glasses to the top – the lovely pink foam will rise from the syrup and the berries. A toast to glorious summer!

Heavenly chocolate cups

Makes 10 small portions

This is a truly French dessert. Serve with caution: no-one can be held responsible for their actions after this. And yes, it's really rich.

- 500 ml thick cream
- 250 g good-quality dark chocolate, broken into little pieces
- 5 egg yolks, beaten
- zest of 1 orange, finely grated
- red berries to serve

Put the cream and chocolate into a pot, and stir over medium heat until the cream is warm enough to melt the chocolate. Take off the heat and cool slightly before folding in the egg yolks. Add the zest. Pour into small ramekins and refrigerate. Serve with red berries.

Crème de cassis sorbet with ripe cherries

Serves 10 easily, with some to spare

Bribe the kids to remove the cherry pips ... then they're the ones who end up with purple fingertips!

- 1 kg fresh cherries, stoned
- zest of 1 lime
- 100 g castor sugar
- 1 t vanilla paste
- 50 ml crème de cassis*

Place the stoned cherries in a bag in the freezer for at least three hours. When they have frozen solid, tip them into a food processor together with the zest, castor sugar, vanilla and crème de cassis, and liquidise until smooth. Scoop into a chilled serving dish and return to the freezer.

Remove the sorbet from the freezer a few minutes before serving. Wonderfully exciting with a glass of bubbly!

* For something different, replace the crème de cassis with grappa.

Autumn

When I think of figs, two special places and seasons come to mind: Cape Town in autumn when my mother would serve us the honey-sweet Cape figs of her youth; and Charroux at the end of summer, where dark-purple figs hang from age-old gnarled trees.

Autumn desserts are shiny caramel-coloured tartes tatin and ochre-stained pears cooked in wine-soaked saffron, redolent of the dusty smells of Moroccan souks. In the background, just a hint of the smoky smell of fireplaces that gently reminds us of the coming winter.

I hope you take huge pleasure from these desserts during this, the slowest of seasons.

Apple & walnut tarts

This is a lovely autumn dessert. In the Auvergne, the apples are in season then. And of course it's walnut country!

- 150 g butter at room temperature, plus extra for greasing
- 150 g castor sugar
- 2 eggs
- 1 t vanilla paste
- 150 g self-raising flour
- 75 g walnuts, chopped
- 3 ripe apples, peeled and thinly sliced
- 50 g icing sugar
- vanilla ice cream to serve

Preheat the oven to 180 deg C/Gas 4. Whisk the butter and castor sugar together until they are a lovely light colour and totally foamy. Add the eggs and the vanilla paste, and mix really well. Add the flour and blend well. Fold the walnuts into the batter.

Butter six little tart moulds and spoon the batter into them. Divide the apple slices among the tarts and arrange them on top of the batter.

Bake for about 20 minutes, remove from the oven and sprinkle the icing sugar over them, and then return to the oven for about 10 minutes to caramelise slightly. Serve with a scoop of vanilla ice cream.

Autumn cake with berries

Serves 10, with possible seconds

This is so good that all my friends have tasted it at least twice!

Batter
- 180 g soft butter, plus extra for greasing
- 500 g castor sugar
- 3 eggs
- 2 egg yolks
- 1 t vanilla paste
- 350 g self-raising flour
- 1 small pinch of salt
- 150 ml milk
- thick cream to serve

Recipe continues overleaf

Preheat the oven to 180 deg C/Gas 4. Line a large bread tin with buttered paper and grease it well.

To make the batter, beat the butter and castor sugar until creamy and pale. Add the eggs, one at a time, and beat thoroughly before adding the yolks for extra richness. Add the vanilla paste.

Mix the flour and salt, and stir into the batter alternately with the milk until everything is incorporated and the mixture is smooth. Spoon into the bread tin and bake for about 90 minutes or until a skewer comes out clean. Allow the cake to stand for 15 minutes before tipping it out of the tin.

continues overleaf

Autumn cake with berries

continued

Sauce
- 100 g castor sugar
- 350 ml water
- 1 T honey
- 200 g assorted berries

Meanwhile, prepare the sauce by placing the castor sugar, 350 ml water and the honey into a saucepan. Bring to the boil and reduce until it reaches a syrupy consistency. Add the berries briefly to the sauce before removing them with a slotted spoon and spooning them 'into' the cake.

Reduce the sauce a little more before pouring it over the cake immediately. It's even better if you can manage this while the cake is still warm! Serve with thick cream.

As an alternative, add 2 T of finely grated lemon peel and the juice of two lemons to the cake mixture. Prepare the sauce with the same amount of castor sugar and water, but add 3 T of lemon juice and roughly chopped citrus peels that have been caramelised.

Crème brûlée with burnt honey

The idea for this dessert was shamelessly stolen from a magazine cover I once saw. I've never seen anything more simple or more pretty! I started to demonstrate it during cooking classes in Cape Town and France ... and it turned out to be a favourite. I normally bake this in heat-resistant glasses.

- 350 ml cream
- 175 ml honey
- 2 eggs, plus two extra yolks, whisked
- 50 ml water

Preheat the oven to 180 deg C/Gas 4. Pour the cream into a pot, add 50 ml of the honey and heat until steaming. Do not boil. Let it cool and whisk it into the egg mixture. Pour into ovenproof ramekins and bake in a bain-marie for about 30 minutes.

Bring the rest of the honey to the boil with 50 ml water, and pour on top of the cooked custards. Serve immediately.

Clafoutis with figs

This is a pleasant and light tart from the Auvergne, to be enjoyed in the late afternoon with a glass of rosé.

- 250 cake flour
- 125 g castor sugar
- pinch of salt
- 4 eggs
- 1 t vanilla paste
- 500 ml boiled milk, cooled
- 2 T Stroh rum
- 12 ripe figs
- butter for greasing
- icing sugar for garnish

Preheat the oven to 200 deg C/Gas 6. Mix together the flour, castor sugar and salt. Beat in the eggs, one at a time, and add the vanilla paste. Using a spatula, fold the milk and Stroh rum into the mixture.

Spread the figs over the bottom of a well-buttered cake tin. Pour the batter over the figs and bake for about 35 minutes. Dust with some icing sugar before serving hot or cold. Lovely!

Autumn fruit salad

The idea for an unseasonal fruit salad came from a collection of recipes by Roald Dahl. I just love the thought! Start the day before.

- 250 g pitted prunes
- 150 g sweet raisins
- 150 ml port
- 1 cinnamon stick
- 1 star anise
- 250 g dried peaches
- 150 ml Cointreau
- 2 ripe oranges, peeled
- 4 crispy apples, peeled
- 250 g dates, seeded
- 125 g flaked almonds, roasted

Soak the prunes and raisins in the port overnight with the cinnamon and star anise. Soak the peaches overnight in the Cointreau.

The next day, cook each fruit in its soaking juices until most of the liquid has evaporated and the fruit is tender. You can add more liquid if necessary.

Remove the pith from the oranges and slice the wedges from the membranes. Slice the apples and core them. Toss the prunes, raisins, dates, oranges and apples together, garnish with the almonds and serve.

Pears in red wine & honey

My mom's recipe for red-wine pears is the one most of us grew up with ... a delicious wine sauce smelling of cinnamon and cloves. Recently I saw a recipe for red fruit with honey and brown sugar and ... voila!

- 6 firm pears
- 750 ml fruity red wine
- 100 ml honey
- 100 g brown sugar
- vanilla to taste ... I like using vanilla paste or scraped vanilla beans
- crème fraîche to serve

Peel the pears, leaving the stalks intact. Combine the wine, honey, brown sugar and vanilla in a large pot. Bring to the boil and simmer until the sugar has dissolved.

Add the pears, placing them upright. Poach slowly until tender, about 15 minutes. Remove the pears from the pot, and reduce the wonderful wine sauce until it has a syrupy consistency.

Serve each pear with a spoonful of syrup dribbled over it and a scoop of crème fraîche.

Luxe apple pies in custard crust

A glorious way to serve these after-dinner snacks is to place a tot measure of Calvados in an elegant little glass on the plate next to the tiny puffs. I love the surprise factor!

- 1 sheet puff pastry, thawed
- butter for greasing
- 1 T castor sugar
- 250 g Mascarpone
- 1 t vanilla paste
- 2 eggs, whisked
- 6 baby apples

Preheat the oven to 220 deg C/Gas 7. With a cookie cutter, cut six small rounds of pastry and place them in greased muffin pans.

In a mixing bowl, fold the castor sugar into the Mascarpone. Gently add the vanilla paste and eggs. Spoon a dollop of this creamy mixture into the middle of each pastry round, and place a tiny apple on top.

Bake immediately for about 25 minutes or until the pastry is a lovely caramel colour. Serve immediately.

Warm rhubarb

Most of our grandparents grew up with rhubarb, and I think it's high time that it be restored to its rightful place as a divine dessert. I sometimes spoon a little cooked rhubarb into ramekins as a sharp little reminder of tastes past, before adding the rest of the ingredients for a crème brûlée. Fantastic!

- 1 bunch rhubarb
- 100 ml fruity white wine
- 100 ml water
- 125 g castor sugar
- 125 ml thick cream or yoghurt to serve

Cut off the rhubarb leaves and wash the stems. Cut the stems into 8 cm lengths.

Put the wine and an equal amount of water in a pot, dissolve the castor sugar in the liquid, add the rhubarb and cook until soft. Remove the rhubarb from the pot and reduce the liquid until it becomes syrupy. Reheat the rhubarb in the syrup and serve warm with a scoop of thick cream or yoghurt.

Serves 6

This is a rich-looking and delicious-tasting dessert that is reminiscent of long, dusty journeys through exotic countries …

- 375 ml Noble Late Harvest wine
- 500 ml water
- 50 g castor sugar
- 2 cinnamon sticks
- 1 t vanilla paste
- 10 ml saffron
- zest of 3 ripe oranges
- 6 pears, peeled and with stems intact
- double cream to serve

Bring 500 ml water and the wine to the boil in a pot big enough to hold six pears. Add the castor sugar and stir gently until it has dissolved. Add the cinnamon sticks, vanilla paste, saffron and orange zest. Add the pears and turn down the heat slightly. Allow the liquid to simmer gently until the pears are cooked and soft, but still firm.

Remove the pears from the pot and keep aside. Reduce the liquid until it is a glossy, rich syrup. Spoon the syrup over the pears and serve with a dollop of double cream.

Fresh figs with Gorgonzola

Another of my favourite fruity desserts!

- butter for greasing
- 6 ripe figs
- 50 ml honey
- 75 g castor sugar
- 125 ml rosé wine
- 1 t vanilla paste
- 250 g Gorgonzola, cut into slices

Preheat the oven to 180 deg C/Gas 4. Butter an ovenproof dish. Break open the figs and place them face-up in the dish. Spoon a little honey on top of each fig. Place the figs in the oven for about 10 minutes and then remove.

Meanwhile, in a skillet, melt the castor sugar in the rosé wine , add the vanilla paste and reduce the mixture until it reaches a syrupy consistency. Remove from the heat.

Place each fig on a small plate, add a generous slice of Gorgonzola and spoon the warm syrup over the fig and cheese. Fabulously decadent!

Serves 8

Serve warm and wobbly.

- butter for greasing
- 1 sheet ready-made short pastry, thawed
- 9 eggs
- 350 g castor sugar
- zest of 2 lemons
- juice of 5 lemons
- 250 ml thick cream
- 75 g icing sugar

Preheat the oven to 180 deg C/Gas 4. Grease a flan tin with a removable base, and fold the pastry into it. Gently use your knuckles to ease the dough into the corners, allowing a small overhang (don't trim it off). Line with buttered paper and fill with baking beans, dry lentils or dry rice. Bake for about 10 minutes, remove from the oven and lift away the paper and 'filling'.

Trim the dough and return to the oven for 10 more minutes, then take it out and turn the oven down to 120 deg C/Gas 1.

In the meantime, whisk the eggs with the castor sugar and zest until light and creamy. Stir in the lemon juice and then gently fold in the cream. Remove any froth before pouring the mixture into the hot pastry case. Bake for about 30 minutes or until the filling has set.

As you take the tart out of the oven, switch on the grill. Sieve the icing sugar over the tart and slide it briefly under the hot grill to caramelise. Serve immediately.

Pancakes with plum compote

When we were students, we only ever entertained if we could do pancakes – with various stuffings. This is a very successful and sweet one.

Compote
- 800 g small plums, seeded and halved
- 150 g castor sugar
- 2 cinnamon sticks
- 2 star anise
- 1 t vanilla paste

Recipe continues overleaf

To make the compote, place the plums in a pan and sprinkle with the castor sugar. Allow the plums to stand for about an hour to extract the juices.

Place the pan on the stove and add the cinnamon sticks, star anise and vanilla paste. Cover the pan and cook over a gentle heat for about 10 minutes. The plums must be soft and the juice syrupy when you remove the pan from the heat.

continues overleaf

Pancakes with plum compote

continued

Batter

- 2 eggs
- 50 ml sunflower oil, plus extra for greasing
- 250 g self-raising flour
- pinch of salt
- 125 ml milk
- crème fraîche to serve
- ground cinnamon for garnish

Batter

To make the batter, whip the eggs with the oil. Add the flour, salt and milk, and mix well. Set the batter aside for about 30 minutes to rest.

Pour a little oil in a crepe pan or skillet over a moderate heat, and spoon a small ladle of batter into the middle of the pan. Twist the pan in a circular movement to cover the bottom of the pan with the batter. Cook the pancake for about 2 minutes on each side, turning with a metal spatula. Repeat until all the batter has been used.

Place a dessert spoon of the compote in the middle of the pancake, fold it over and spoon a dollop of crème fraîche on top. Garnish with a sprinkle of ground cinnamon and serve.

Melon & black fig salad

A fresh and novel alternative to a fruit salad.

- 1 melon, seeded and quartered
- 4 ripe black figs
- 125 ml medium sherry
- 75 g pistachios, peeled and roasted
- crème fraîche to serve

Slice the flesh of the melon into smallish chunks and place in a bowl. Break the figs into quarters and toss them with the melon. Mix the sherry into the fruit and refrigerate the salad for an hour or two.

Sprinkle the pistachios over the salad before serving with a dollop of crème fraîche.

Tarte tatin

The Tatin sisters ran a restaurant in Lamotte-Beuvron at the beginning of the last century and, according to legend, one of the old girls dropped the tart as she was putting it in the oven ... hence baking it upside down. The absolutely delicious result is butter, sugar and apple juice all coming together in the most divine caramel. I just love this story and am constantly dropping stuff in the hope ...

- 125 g unsalted butter, diced
- 11 Golden Delicious apples, peeled and each sliced into six wedges
- 550 g castor sugar
- 2 T water
- 125 ml crème fraîche
- 1 sheet puff pastry, thawed
- cream to serve

Preheat the oven to 180 deg C/Gas 4. Use a tablespoon of the butter to grease a baking tray, and neatly pack the sliced apple wedges onto the tray. Sprinkle 50 g of the castor sugar evenly over the apple wedges and bake/dry them in the oven for about 1½ hours, or until the apples turn a light caramel colour. Quickly remove them from the tray – they tend to stick!

Meanwhile, melt the rest of the castor sugar in a saucepan with 2 T of water. Wait until the caramel boils in lovely, big bubbles before you add the crème fraîche. Beware of the steam! Keep stirring until the extra moisture has reduced, then stir the remaining butter into the sauce. It keeps the caramel from becoming too sticky.

Pour the caramel into a round springform cake tin and let it cool to room temperature. Pack the apple wedges into the caramel in overlapping concentric circles. Cover the fruit with the pastry, tucking it under the edge of the cake tin. Prick with a fork. Put the tin onto a baking tray ... the tart tends to leak a little ... and bake for 45 minutes at 200 deg C/Gas 6 or until the pastry turns a golden, caramel colour.

Remove from the oven and tip the baking tin over deftly – don't burn yourself! Serve still slightly warm with a dollop of cream.

Pears & prunes poached in red wine with crème de cassis

This is a wonderful recipe that hails from Burgundy.

- 6 firm ripe pears, peeled
- 10 whole fresh prunes
- 750 ml Pinot Noir wine
- 4 T castor sugar
- 200 ml crème de cassis
- 1 cinnamon stick
- 100 g hazelnuts, peeled and roasted
- vanilla ice cream to serve

Put the pears and prunes in a pan and cover with the wine. Add some water if needed. Add the castor sugar, crème de cassis and cinnamon stick. Cook over a low heat until the pears are tender but still firm.

Transfer the pears to a serving platter. Reduce the remaining liquid, with the whole prunes still in the juice, until it reaches a syrupy consistency. Remove the cinnamon stick and spoon the prunes and syrup over the pears.

Toss the hazelnuts lightly into the fruit. Serve with a scoop of vanilla ice cream.

Fig & almond tart

Serves 8

This dessert was first made during a cook's tour in Charroux when a local farmer brought us a basketful of figs. A lovely dessert or as an accompaniment to a glass of cold white wine.

Shortcrust pastry
- 125 g butter
- 100 g icing sugar
- 255 g cake flour
- vanilla paste
- 2 large egg yolks
- 2 T cold milk
- zest of ½ lemon

Frangipane
- 255 g unsalted butter
- 255 g castor sugar
- 285 g ground almonds
- 2 large eggs, lightly beaten
- vanilla paste
- 1 T grappa

Recipe continues overleaf

First prepare the shortcrust pastry.

To make the pastry, mix the sugar and butter in a bowl until it has a creamy consistency. Add the flour, vanilla paste, egg yolks as well as the milk and mix well. Fold the lemon zest into the mixture and rest it in the fridge for about an hour. Then line a 28 cm loose-bottomed tin with the pastry and blindbake for 12 minutes at 180 deg C/Gas 4.

To make the frangipane, cream together the butter and castor sugar. Add the rest of the ingredients and stir together. Then cool the mixture in the fridge.

continues overleaf

Fig & almond tart

continued

Fruit

- 30 g castor sugar
- 2 T water
- 12 whole figs*
- 2 sprigs thyme
- zest of 1 orange
- Mascarpone or crème fraîche to serve

Fruit

To prepare the fruit, heat the castor sugar and 2 T of water to form a syrup.

Spoon the frangipane into the pastry shell. Slice the figs and arrange them on the frangipane. Drizzle the syrup over the fruit, and sprinkle with the thyme and orange zest.

Bake for about 40 minutes at 180 deg C/Gas 4 or until golden brown. Lovely served with a dollop of Mascarpone or crème fraîche.

* *You could also use any other seeded fruit such as nectarines, plums, peaches or apricots.*

Winter

Oranges and honey are reminiscent of the welcome warmth of log fires in old fireplaces, enjoyed from deep leather armchairs after a short, harshly cold winter day. The smell of oranges from the basket in the pantry is lightly touched by a hint of cinnamon and honey from something alluring in the oven.

My winter's wish is that you will turn on your ovens, butter ovenproof dishes and take great joy in these soul-warming winter desserts. Serve them with lashings of freshly made custard and heaps of love.

And do remember that a spoonful of honey can only serve you well! Enjoy.

Poppy seed & citrus cake

Another family favourite that has its regular place in the 'What cake do we have for the weekend?' line-up.

Batter

- 125 g butter, plus extra for greasing
- 250 g castor sugar
- 2 eggs
- zest of 1 large lemon
- 375 ml self-raising flour, plus extra for flouring
- 125 ml milk
- 2 t vanilla paste
- 1 t ground cinnamon
- 125 ml poppy seeds

Sauce

- juice of 1 lemon
- 250 g castor sugar
- 250 ml water
- zest of 2 oranges
- zest of 2 lemons
- zest of 2 limes

Preheat the oven to 180 deg C/Gas 4, and butter and flour a round cake tin. It is also a good idea to line the tin with a round of buttered paper.

To make the batter, cream the butter and castor sugar before adding the eggs, one at a time. Beat well. Stir in the zest, flour, milk, vanilla paste, cinnamon and poppy seeds, and mix really well.

Spoon the dough into the cake tin and bake for about 35 minutes or until a skewer comes out clean. Allow the cake to rest for a while before turning it out onto a cooling rack.

To make the sauce, combine the lemon juice, castor sugar and 250 ml water in a small pot. Bring to a gentle boil and allow the sugar to melt before adding all the zest. Keep reducing the liquid until it is wonderfully syrupy and the zest is completely glazed and almost transparent.

Place the cake on a serving platter and spoon the very-warm syrup over it. To decorate, pile the zest in a heap in the middle of the cake.

Baked plums with crème de cassis & honey

I love making this really easy dessert in winter.

- butter for greasing
- 6 ripe plums, seeded and halved
- 125 ml crème de cassis
- 75 ml honey
- 1 T ground cinnamon
- 2 star anise
- Mascarpone to serve

Preheat the oven to 180 deg C/Gas 4. Butter an ovenproof dish and place the plums into the dish face-up. Pour the crème de cassis liberally over the plums. Spoon a little of the honey onto each plum and dust with the ground cinnamon.

Place the star anise in the dish, cover and put in the oven for about 10 minutes. Remove the cover and bake for another 10 minutes.

Remove the plums from the dish, drain the excess liquid into a small skillet, add the rest of the honey and bring to a gentle simmer. Cook until the sauce forms a glossy syrup.

Place the plums on six small plates, spoon the syrup over them and serve with a dollop of Mascarpone.

Malva pudding

This is on special request for my friends at the breathtaking guesthouse, Clos du Léthé, in Uzès, close to Avignon ... a classic dessert from South Africa.

Sauce
- 250 ml thick cream
- 250 ml milk
- 1 t vanilla paste
- 125 g butter, plus extra for greasing
- 125 g castor sugar

Batter
- 250 g castor sugar
- 50 g butter
- 1 egg
- 250 g self-raising flour
- pinch of salt
- 250 ml milk
- 1 t wine vinegar
- 1 T smooth apricot jam
- vanilla ice cream to serve

Preheat the oven to 180 deg C/Gas 4 and grease an ovenproof pudding dish.

To make the sauce, combine the cream, milk, vanilla paste, butter and castor sugar in a saucepan, and heat while stirring gently. As soon as it starts to boil, remove from the heat.

To make the batter, combine the castor sugar and butter in a blender. Add the egg and blend well. Combine the flour and salt, and add along with the milk. Stir the wine vinegar into the jam and add to the mixture. Blend thoroughly, and then spoon the dough into the pudding dish. Bake for about 35 minutes or until a skewer comes out clean.

Gently reheat the sauce and immediately spoon it over the pudding. Allow the sauce enough time to soak into the pudding before serving it with a scoop of vanilla ice cream. Utterly delicious!

Fig & nut cake with creamy coffee icing

Batter
- 125 g butter, plus extra for greasing
- 500 g sugar
- 2 eggs
- 375 g self-raising flour
- 1 t salt
- 1 t ground cinnamon
- ¼ t ground cloves
- 500 g dried figs, lightly stewed in 250 ml water and chopped into small cubes (don't throw the water away!)
- 125 ml milk
- 125 g walnuts, chopped
- 2 t vanilla paste

Icing
- 750 g icing sugar, sifted
- 125 g softened butter
- 1 T coffee essence
- 1 T milk
- 1 t vanilla paste

When my son was young we used to bake a cake every Friday afternoon. This was an absolute favourite.

Preheat the oven to 180 deg C/Gas 4. To make the batter, cream the butter and sugar until light in colour. Add the eggs, one at a time, and beat well.

Sift all the dry ingredients together and fold into the egg mixture, alternating with the leftover liquid from the stewed figs and the milk. Fold in the figs, walnuts and vanilla paste.

Pour the batter into a buttered cake tin and bake for about 80 minutes or until a skewer comes out clean. Remove from the oven and allow to rest a little before turning the cake out onto a cooling rack.

When the cake is cold, make the icing. Beat the icing sugar, butter, coffee essence, milk and vanilla paste together until smooth and creamy, and spread over the cake. Enjoy with a glass of sweet wine.

Honey & cheese cake

This is a family recipe that has become my son's favourite. My mother had to bake this for his 21st birthday!

Cake

- 75 g butter, room temperature
- 250 g castor sugar
- 3 eggs
- 350 g self-raising flour
- 1 t vanilla paste
- 175 ml full cream milk
- 250 g cheddar cheese, finely grated

Sauce

- 75 g butter
- 150 ml honey

Pre-heat the oven to 180 degrees/Gas 4. Butter an ovenproof baking dish. Whisk the butter and the sugar until it is light and fluffy. Add the eggs and whisk well. Sift the flour into the mixture, add the vanilla and pour the milk into the batter while you are whisking it. Bake the cake for about 25 minutes or until a skewer comes out clean.

While the cake is baking, make the sauce. Spoon the honey into the butter and heat together until the butter and honey have melted and formed a lovely, glossy sauce. Remove the sauce from the heat when the cake is ready.

Remove the cake from the oven, pour the piping hot sauce over it while it is still warm and then sprinkle with the grated cheese. Eat immediately. This is utterly delicious!

Chocolate pots

Serves 6

An old favourite looking all new in individual moulds. I always find comfort in remembered tastes …

Batter
- 75 g butter, plus extra for greasing
- 180 g castor sugar
- 2 eggs
- 2 T cocoa powder
- pinch of salt
- 250 g self-raising flour
- 125 ml milk
- ½ t vanilla paste

Sauce
- 250 g brown sugar
- 2 T cocoa powder
- 1 t vanilla paste
- 125 ml boiling water
- vanilla ice cream to serve

Preheat the oven to 180 deg C/Gas 4. To make the batter, whip the butter and castor sugar together until pale and fluffy. Add the eggs, one at a time, beating constantly.

Sift the cocoa powder, salt and flour together and fold into the mixture. Mix well. Add the milk a little at a time, making sure to blend the mixture properly. Add the vanilla paste.

To make the sauce, stir all the sauce ingredients together in a bowl with 325 ml of boiling water. Keep stirring until the brown sugar dissolves.

Butter six ramekins and pour a little sauce into each. Follow with the batter – the ramekins should be about three-quarters full. Bake for about 30 minutes. The sauce will gradually bubble gently to the top of each pudding.

Serve with a dollop of vanilla ice cream.

Orange pudding from Ouma Mollie

Batter
- 125 g castor sugar
- 100 g butter, plus extra for greasing
- 50 ml sunflower oil
- pinch of salt
- 1 egg
- 250 g self-raising flour, sifted
- 1 medium orange, peeled and seeded

Sauce
- 125 g castor sugar
- 250 ml water
- juice of 2 oranges
- 1 T orange zest
- 1 T good-quality brandy
- crème anglaise or vanilla ice cream to serve

Oranges are the main crop in the Gamtoos Valley in the Eastern Cape, where my grandmother was the Dutch Reformed dominee's wife. She called this her 'own concoction' and advised that, as this is a 'small pudding', it is better to either double or treble the ingredients for a big family.

Preheat the oven to 180 deg C/Gas 4. To make the batter, blend the castor sugar and butter until creamy. Add the oil, salt and egg, and mix well. Add the flour. Break the flesh of the orange into tiny pieces over the mixing bowl to catch all the juice, and fold it all into the dough.

Spoon the mixture into a greased ovenproof baking dish. Bake for about 30 minutes or until a skewer comes out clean.

Meanwhile, make the sauce. Pour 250 ml water and the castor sugar into a saucepan and bring to a slow boil, stirring until the sugar has melted. Add the orange juice and zest, and reduce for about six minutes or until syrupy. Add the brandy and pour the syrup over the lovely, crusty cake as it comes out of the oven.

Serve with crème anglaise (see p. 136) or a scoop of vanilla ice cream.

Fabulous coffee cake

This is my favourite cake.
And one my dear mother
had to make on my birthday
every year ... that is, after the
specially requested bowl of
tripe! No logic whatsoever.

- 200 g butter, plus extra for greasing
- 250 g castor sugar
- 3 eggs
- 375 g self-raising flour
- pinch of salt
- 100 g sugar
- 250 ml strong black coffee
- Cognac to taste
- 1 t vanilla paste
- 250 ml thick cream
- handful of flaked almonds, lightly roasted

Preheat the oven to 190 deg C/Gas 5. Grease a 20 cm ring form or normal cake tin. In a blender, cream the butter and castor sugar until light and airy. Add the eggs, one at a time, and beat in thoroughly. Gently fold the flour and salt into the mixture.

Spoon into the cake tin and bake for about 30 minutes or until a skewer comes out clean. Remove from the oven and allow to rest for a couple of minutes before tipping onto a cooling rack.

In a pan, dissolve the sugar in the coffee and add the Cognac to taste. Place the cooled cake on a cake stand and gently pour the coffee syrup over the cake, completely drenching it.

Combine the vanilla and cream and whip the mixture until it forms soft peaks. Spoon the mixture over the coffee cake and garnish with the almonds. You might be tempted to enjoy this with a small tumbler of Cognac!

Roly-poly with apricot confit

Serves a family of 6, easily

This jammy, saucy pudding has been a family favourite for as long as I can remember. My brother, Gert Renier, regularly made this for 'something sweet' after a Sunday lunch.

Batter
- 250 g butter (of which 125 g is diced), plus extra for greasing
- 500 g self-raising flour, plus extra for flouring
- 1 t vanilla paste
- 125 ml milk
- 250 g thick, glossy apricot jam, or to taste
- 500 ml water
- 250 g castor sugar

Crème anglaise
- 500 ml milk
- 6 egg yolks
- 125 g sugar
- vanilla paste to taste

Preheat the oven to 180 deg C/Gas 4. To make the batter, rub 125 g butter into the flour with your fingertips. Add the vanilla paste and milk, and fold together to form a soft dough.

Roll the dough into a square on a floured board. The dough must be thinnish – about 2 mm to 3 mm. Spread liberally with the jam, then roll up like a Swiss roll and place in a buttered pie dish.

Pour 500 ml cold water into the dish. Sprinkle the castor sugar over the dough and then add the 125 g of diced butter. Bake for 90 minutes or until a glorious caramel colour. Cut into slices.

To make the crème anglaise, bring the milk to the boil in a saucepan, and then remove from the heat. Meanwhile, beat the egg yolks with the sugar until frothy. Slowly pour the mixture into the still-warm milk, whisking furiously as you go.

Return the mixture to the saucepan and cook over a very low heat, stirring constantly, until it coats the back of a spoon. Add the vanilla paste, set aside to cool and then serve with the pudding.

Spicy citrus cake

*This must-have cake is
spectacularly easy to make!*

- 500 g self-raising flour
- 175 g castor sugar
- ½ t salt
- 125 ml sunflower oil
- 5 eggs, separated
- 200 ml water
- zest of 1 orange
- zest of 2 limes
- 1 t vanilla paste
- 1 t ground cinnamon
- butter for greasing
- icing sugar for dusting

Preheat the oven to 180 deg C/Gas 4. Mix together the flour, castor sugar and salt. Add the oil, beaten yolks and 200 ml cold water, and whisk well. Beat the egg whites until they form soft peaks, and fold into the batter with the orange zest, lime zest, vanilla paste and cinnamon.

Pour the batter into a large, buttered springform pan and bake for 1 hour or until a skewer comes out clean. Let the cake cool before removing it from the pan, and then dust with some icing sugar.

Steamed honey & cinnamon pudding

This is truly a winter's pudding and should be served with a proper crème anglaise.

- 60 ml honey, warmed
- 120 g butter, plus extra for greasing
- 60 g castor sugar
- 1 t vanilla paste
- 2 eggs, whisked
- 125 g self-raising flour
- zest of 1 lemon
- 1 t ground cinnamon
- 75 g pecan nuts, chopped
- crème anglaise to serve

Fill a large cooking pot with water and bring to the boil. Grease a pudding bowl with butter and pour the warmed honey into the bowl. Swirl it around gently, covering the entire bowl with a thin layer of honey.

In the meantime, beat together the butter, castor sugar and vanilla paste until it is light yellow and foamy. Gradually beat in the eggs. Gently fold in the flour, lemon rind, cinnamon and pecan nuts.

Spoon the batter into the pudding bowl and cover tightly with a cloth tied with a piece of string. Immerse the bowl in the boiling water, reduce the heat to low and allow the pudding to steam for 1½ hours.

Once cooked, allow the pudding to cool a bit before you turn it out. Serve with a jug of crème anglaise (see p. 136).

Spicy caramelised nuts

The best! My mom does them in the winter to stave off the cold. It works every year ...

- 50 ml olive oil
- 300 g mixed nuts
- 125 g castor sugar
- ¼ t salt
- 5 ml ground cumin seeds
- 5 ml ground coriander seeds
- 5 cardamom pods, peeled and ground

Heat the oil, add the nuts, and sprinkle castor sugar and salt over the mixture. Cook and stir until the sugar has melted and the nuts are golden.

Meanwhile, mix the spices in a bowl. As soon as the nuts are ready, scrape them into the spices and toss quickly. Tip out onto a baking tray lined with buttered paper and, using a fork, separate any that have stuck together. Leave to cool before serving.

Orange cake with lime Mascarpone

Serves 16, with plenty left over for you

This is an excellent cake. I serve it in winter with a glass of Sauternes or any of our local dessert wines. The batter makes 2 x 20 cm cakes and they keep well in a sealed container.

- 2 large oranges
- butter for greasing
- flour for flouring
- 6 eggs
- 550 g sugar
- 1 t baking powder
- 550 g ground almonds
- 10 g ground cinnamon
- zest and juice of 2 limes
- 250 g Mascarpone

Place the oranges whole into a saucepan with enough water to cover them. Simmer for 1 hour or until the oranges are completely tender. You will need to change the simmering water up to three times to get rid of any traces of bitterness. Cut the oranges in half, remove the seeds, and purée the flesh and peels in a blender.

Preheat the oven to 180 deg C/Gas 4. Butter and flour two 20 cm springform tins and line the bottoms with baking paper. Beat the eggs and 500 g of the sugar until the mixture is pale and thick.

Combine the baking powder, almonds and cinnamon, and stir into the egg mixture. Then fold it into the orange purée.

Pour the batter into the prepared tins and bake on the centre shelf for 60 minutes or until a skewer inserted into the centre of the cakes comes out clean. Turn out the cakes onto a cooling rack.

While the cakes are cooling, make the lime Mascarpone by combining the rest of the sugar with the lime zest, lime juice and Mascarpone. Adjust the lime juice and sugar if necessary.

Serve the cake in wedges with a spoonful of lime Mascarpone and, if you like, some mixed berries.

Crêpes with honey & pine nuts

I found this recipe in an old French cookbook and I've loved it ever since.

- 60 g butter, plus extra for greasing
- 100 g cake flour
- 2 large eggs
- 1 T sugar
- 200 ml milk
- 100 g honey
- 250 ml thick cream, completely chilled
- 4 egg yolks, whipped very well
- few drops of pastis*
- 125 g pine nuts, roasted

Heat the butter in a pan and allow it to brown slightly to achieve that fabulous nut-butter colour and taste. With an electric mixer, combine the flour, eggs and sugar. Slowly pour the milk and nut-butter in a stream into the batter, a little at a time, whisking constantly. Pour the batter through a strainer and allow it to rest for about 1 hour.

While the batter is resting, warm the honey over a low heat. It must not boil. The moment it has liquefied, remove it from the heat. Whip the very cold cream until it has formed stiff peaks and is very well aerated. By hand, fold the honey, egg yolks and pastis* into the cream. Refrigerate immediately.

Place a small crêpe pan or skillet onto moderate heat. Drop a small piece of butter in the pan and melt it. Stir the batter a little and spoon a ladleful into the middle of the pan. Twist the pan in a circular movement to cover the bottom of the pan with the batter.

Cook the crêpes for about 2 minutes on each side, turning with a metal spatula. Repeat until all the batter has been used. Fold the crêpes into quarters, spoon the thick cream and honey glaze on top of each crêpe, garnish with the pine nuts and serve.

* This is optional. (I love it, though!)

Coffee & hazelnut cake with golden syrup sauce

You can use walnuts or almonds instead of hazelnuts in this lovely tea cake.

Sauce
- 50 g unsalted butter, plus extra for greasing
- 100 ml golden syrup
- 125 g Demerara sugar
- 125 g hazelnuts, peeled and roasted

Recipe continues overleaf

Preheat the oven to 180 deg C/Gas 4. To make the sauce, put the butter, syrup and Demerara sugar in a small saucepan and stir over a low heat until the sugar has melted and the sauce begins to caramelise.

Add the hazelnuts to the sauce and spoon it into the bottom of a buttered cake tin. Allow the sauce to cool completely before spooning the batter mixture into the cake tin.

continues overleaf

Coffee & hazelnut cake with golden syrup sauce

continued

Batter
- 125 g butter, room temperature
- 250 g castor sugar
- 1 t vanilla paste
- 125 g hazelnuts, peeled, roasted and chopped
- 2 eggs, separated
- 350 g self-raising flour
- 125 ml milk
- 2 T espresso
- thick cream to serve

To make the batter, beat the butter and castor sugar until the mixture is really light and fluffy. Add the vanilla paste* and fold the hazelnuts into the batter. Add the egg yolks, one at a time, and mix thoroughly. Sift the flour into the bowl. Add the milk and espresso gradually and mix until everything is well combined.

Whisk the egg whites until they are quite stiff before folding them into the batter. Spoon the batter evenly into the cake tin on top of the cooled syrup. Bake for about 1 hour or until a skewer comes out clean.

Allow the cake to cool before running a knife around the edge of the tin and turning the cake out onto a serving plate. This is lovely served with a dollop of thick cream.

* See page 157

Baked banana & orange pudding

This is a delicious, self-saucing pudding that my grandmother, Mollie, was served directly after she gave birth to her youngest daughter, my aunt Anita. Ouma loved her snacks!

- 100 g butter, plus extra for greasing
- 250 g castor sugar
- 4 eggs, separated
- juice of 1 lemon
- 1 t vanilla paste
- 250 g self-raising flour
- 75 ml milk
- zest of 1 unwaxed orange
- 4 bananas, peeled and sliced

Preheat the oven to 180 deg C/Gas 4 and butter an ovenproof dish. Whisk the butter and castor sugar together until the mixture is light and foamy. Whisk the egg yolks, and add the lemon juice and vanilla paste. Mix really well and add the flour. Continue mixing while slowly adding the milk. Fold the orange zest into the mixture.

Whisk the egg whites until they form soft peaks before folding them into the batter. Place the sliced banana into the ovenproof dish and spoon the batter on top. Bake the cake in a bain-marie until a skewer comes out clean, about 35 minutes.

Tea cake with glazed fruit

- 100 g sultanas
- 75 ml sweet sherry
- 225 g almonds, peeled and roughly chopped
- 225 g glacé orange and lemon peel, chopped
- 2 glacé dried green figs, chopped
- 10 glacé cherries, halved
- 200 g pine nuts, roasted
- 150 g dark chocolate, chopped
- 150 g castor sugar
- 125 g self-raising flour
- 1 t ground cinnamon
- 1 t allspice powder
- 3 cardamom pods, peeled and ground
- 50 g unsalted butter, plus extra for greasing
- 3 eggs
- 3 T honey, melted
- heaps of different types of whole glacé fruit to decorate
- thick cream to serve

A lighter and more colourful version of the English fruit cake. I really like this one ... Start the day before.

Preheat the oven to 180 deg C/Gas 4. Generously grease a medium cake tin, preferably one that is loose-bottomed. Some buttered paper might also help!

Soak the sultanas in the sherry overnight. Place the sultanas, any remaining sherry, the almonds, orange and lemon peel, figs, cherries, pine nuts and chocolate in a large bowl. Add the castor sugar and mix carefully.

Sift the flour, cinnamon and allspice in a separate bowl. Add the cardamom. Tip these dry ingredients into the fruit and sugar mixture.

Whisk the butter and eggs until light and foamy. Fold them into the fruit, nut and sugar mixture. Add the honey. Gently fold all the ingredients together until the mixture is lovely and shiny.

Pour the doughy mixture into the cake tin and bake for about 50 minutes or until a skewer comes out clean. Allow the cake to cool slightly before removing it from the tin.

Place the cake on a cake stand and, if you like, sprinkle a little sweet sherry or even some brandy onto the still-warm cake. Decorate with the lovely glacé fruit and serve with thick cream.

Glossary

bain-marie: pan with simmering water with a bowl suspended in it

blinis: small panfried crumpets

clafoutis: black cherries baked covered in a fairly thick pancake batter

compote: a preparation of either dried or fresh fruits cooked in a sugar syrup

coulis: a liquid purée of fruit

crème anglaise: custard

crème fraîche: a cream to which a lactic acid has been added which thickens the cream, and gives it a distinctive sharp flavour without souring the cream

crêpe: thin pancake

Demerara sugar: natural brown sugar

dollop: scoop

frangipane: pastry cream made from milk, sugar, flour, eggs, butter, crushed macaroons or almonds

Mascarpone: Italian triple cream cheese

poach: lightly boil in wine or water

purée: creaming cooked foods through a sieve or with a food processor

reduce: to concentrate or thicken a sauce by boiling

sabayon: light foam made by whisking egg yolks, wine and sugar together over a gentle heat

saffron: a spice derived from the dried stigma of the saffron crocus; it has a pungent smell and a bitter flavour

sorbet: a water-ice that is softer and more granular than ice cream

soufflé: a light and fluffy baked dish using beaten egg whites

soupçon: a very small amount of something, the merest hint

T: tablespoon

t: teaspoon

vanilla paste: is an easy-to-use replacement for whole vanilla beans. A fairly new product in South Africa but can be found at most delis.

zest: the coloured or outer rind of any citrus fruit

Index

Jellies, salads, pancakes & extras

Autumn fruit salad 90
Champagne jelly with berries 16
Crêpes with honey & pine nuts 146
Griet's banana bread 18
Melon & black fig salad 108
Pancakes with plum compote 104
Panna cotta with basil 36
Spicy caramelised nuts 142

Puddings

Baked banana & orange pudding 152
Malva pudding 124
Orange pudding from Ouma
    Mollie 132
Steamed honey & cinnamon
    pudding 140

Sweet & cheesy

Cheesy cream 46
Fresh figs with Gorgonzola 100
Peaches in white wine syrup
    with Roquefort 56
Ricotta dessert with Cognac
    & citrus zest 70

Tarts & pies

Apple & walnut tarts 80
Banana frangipane 64
Berry tarts with Mascarpone 34
Blueberry pie 52
Cherry clafoutis 62
Clafoutis with figs 88
Fig & almond tart 114
Grape & fennel seed tart 68
Luxe apple pies in custard crust 94
Peach & caramel tarts 26
Tarte au citron 102
Tarte tatin 110